AF429164

Thriving In Your Twenties: A Roadmap to Self-Discovery and Growth

Copyright © 2024 Deandra Rose

All rights reserved. This book or any portion thereof
may not be reproduced or used in any
manner whatsoever without the express written
permission of the publisher except for the use of brief
quotations in a book review.

INTRODUCTION

Welcome to "Thriving in Your Twenties: A Roadmap to Self-Discovery and Growth."

In this book, we'll embark on a journey of self-discovery, delving into topics that will empower you to define your values, set meaningful goals, and take purposeful actions towards a fulfilling future. We'll explore avenues for personal growth, relationships, career development, and more.

Each chapter is designed to provide you with practical tools such as: Key Points, Action Steps, Affirmations, Essential Life Tips, relatable examples, and a touch of humour to guide you along this transformative path. Think of this book as your compass, helping you navigate through the exciting terrain of your twenties.

Why Trust This Roadmap?

The insights and strategies shared in this book are not just theoretical; they're grounded in real-life experiences.

The goal is to equip you with the knowledge and confidence to make informed decisions, embrace change, and step boldly into your future.

So, whether you're seeking guidance on personal development, career choices, relationships, or simply looking for inspiration and motivation to embark on this adventure, you'll find it within these pages.

Let's embark on this transformative journey together. Remember, your twenties are a canvas, and you hold the brush.

It's time to paint a masterpiece!

CONTENT PAGE

CHAPTER

01

EMBRACING YOUR TWENTIES: NAVIGATING THE DECADE OF CHANGE

Understanding the Significance of Your Twenties

Welcome to the Twenties Club! No, we're not talking about parties or dance clubs (although those can be fun too). Your twenties are like the prologue to your blockbuster novel of life. It's the time when you're upgrading from the "Trial Version" to the "Full Experience" of adulthood.

Imagine your twenties as a rollercoaster - sometimes thrilling, occasionally scary, and always a bit disorienting.

Embrace it!

Embracing the Opportunities for Growth and Exploration

Think of your twenties as a buffet of experiences. You've got the whole spread in front of you - higher education, career choices, new cities, and maybe even a unique hobby. This is the time to load up your plate and sample a bit of everything.

Remember, it's okay if you're not entirely sure what you want to be when you grow up. Heck, some are still figuring it out in their thirties! So, seize the day, try new things, and remember that even if it doesn't lead to your dream job, it could lead to a great story.

Setting the Stage for Personal and Professional Development

Alright, let's talk game plan. Picture yourself as the director of your own movie. What's the plot? What are the character arcs? This is the time to set the stage for your future successes and epic plot twists.

Grab a notebook, make a list, and put those dreams on paper. Whether it's conquering a career milestone, travelling the world, or simply mastering the art of cooking something other than instant noodles, your goals are the stars of the show.

Key Takeaways:

- Your twenties are like the prologue to your blockbuster novel of life – thrilling, scary, and occasionally disorienting.
  - Think of this period as a buffet of experiences – load up your plate and sample a bit of everything.
  - Set the stage for your future successes and epic plot twists by defining your goals.

Action Steps:

- Take a moment to envision your dream adventure in your twenties – what does it look like?
- Embrace a new experience or try something completely out of your comfort zone this month.
- Begin outlining a game plan for achieving one of your chosen goals and remember to include a few plot twists for good measure!

ESSENTIAL LIFE TIPS FOR YOUR JOURNEY

- Networking isn't just about business cards – build genuine connections by being authentic and showing interest in others.

- Invest time in honing your soft skills; effective communication and emotional intelligence are your secret weapons.

- Embrace failure as a stepping stone to success; every setback is a lesson pushing you closer to your goals.

- Create a healthy work-life balance; success is not just about the hustle, but also about well-being and happiness.

- Stay curious and never stop learning; the world is evolving, and so should you. Explore new skills and stay adaptable.

EMPOWERING AFFIRMATIONS

- I am constantly evolving and growing, embracing every opportunity for personal development.

- My unique skills and talents are valuable assets, driving me forward in my professional journey.

- I trust the process of life and confidently step out of my comfort zone to reach new heights.

- Challenges are opportunities in disguise, and I tackle them with resilience and a positive mindset.

- I am the architect of my future, creating a life that aligns with my passions and aspirations.

SAY THESE OUT LOUD!

CHAPTER

02

DISCOVERING YOUR TRUE SELF: UNLEASHING YOUR AUTHENTICITY

Embracing Your Identity and Individuality

 You're not here to blend into the background like a potted plant at a garden party. Your individuality is your secret superpower. You're a limited edition, one-of-a-kind masterpiece!

Your quirks, your interests, and even that inexplicable obsession with collecting vintage soda cans – it all makes you, well, you! So, whether you're into knitting neon-coloured scarves for your pet iguana or know the entire script of that obscure 80s movie by heart, own it! Let your flag fly. It's what sets you apart and makes life's tapestry so darn interesting.

In the grand adventure of life, your twenties are like the chapter titled "Quest for Self." It's when you embark on the epic journey of self-discovery. Think of it as your own personal treasure hunt, with the treasure being the most awesome version of yourself.

Try on different hats – figuratively and maybe even literally. Explore new interests, dive into hobbies that pique your curiosity, and yes, even make a few decisions that might end up in the "Learning Experiences" folder. Every mishap is just a plot twist in your hero's journey.

Building Confidence in Your Own Skin

Let's talk confidence, shall we? Confidence isn't about being the loudest person in the room or having the perfect Instagram pose down pat. It's about being comfortable in your own skin, quirks and all. It's that inner glow that radiates when you know you're awesome, just the way you are.

So, rock those mismatched socks like it's a fashion statement. Confidence is the swagger that comes from embracing yourself fully. After all, who needs a superhero cape when you've got the confidence to conquer the world?

Embarking on the wild adventure of discovering your true self in your twenties is like trying to manoeuvre a maze with a blindfold on, armed only with a dimly lit flashlight called "self-awareness." It's a time when you're juggling more existential questions than a philosophy professor on a caffeine bender.

You find yourself pondering life's greatest mysteries, like whether your passion for binge-watching reality TV is a legitimate calling or just a really good excuse to avoid adulting.

Values and beliefs become the stars of your own personal soap opera. You're sorting through them, trying to decide which ones are genuine treasures and which are just knockoff imposters. And let's not even get started on passions.

You're on a mission to unearth what makes your heart do the happy dance, even if it means trying out salsa dancing, interpretive dance, or any other dance that doesn't require a tutu.

But here comes the plot twist: external pressures and expectations swoop in like overbearing relatives at a family gathering.

Suddenly, you're bombarded with questions like, "When are you getting a 'real' job?" or "Why aren't you married yet?" It's like society has a checklist and you're supposed to tick all the boxes, but you've got your list, and it includes things like "master the art of making the perfect grilled cheese sandwich" and "learn how to fold a fitted sheet."

So, you boldly declare, "I am the captain of my own ship, and I'm setting sail for the land of self-discovery!" You sail through choppy waters of judgmental glances and unsolicited advice, armed with the knowledge that your true north is defined by you, not society's compass.

My Personal Experience

As a young Black woman in my twenties, navigating the complexities of self-confidence in today's society has been a journey filled with ups and downs, triumphs and setbacks. From a young age, I grappled with the pressure to conform to societal standards of beauty and success, constantly bombarded with messages that undermined my sense of self-worth. But as I journeyed through life, I discovered the power of embracing my true identity and individuality, despite the external pressures and expectations that sought to define me.

One of the most transformative moments in my journey to building confidence was the realisation that true beauty and worth come from within. In a society that often equates beauty with Eurocentric features and a certain body type, I struggled to see myself reflected in the images and ideals perpetuated by the media. But as I embarked on a journey of self-discovery and self-love, I learned to embrace the beauty of my natural hair, the curves of my body, and the richness of my melanin. I refused to allow society's standards of beauty to dictate my sense of self-worth, choosing instead to celebrate my uniqueness and embrace my true identity.

Furthermore, I learned to silence the voices of doubt and negativity that sought to undermine my confidence. Whether it was the subtle micro-aggressions of everyday life or the overt racism and discrimination I encountered in certain spaces, I refused to internalise the negativity or allow it to dim my light. Instead, I surrounded myself with positive influences and affirmations that uplifted and empowered me, reminding myself of my inherent worth and value as a Black woman.

Another pivotal moment in my journey to building confidence was the realisation that I am more than the sum of my achievements or external validations. In a society that often measures success by material wealth or social status, I refused to define my worth by external metrics or comparisons to others. Instead, I focused on cultivating a sense of inner fulfilment and purpose, pursuing passions and interests that brought me joy and fulfilment, regardless of external recognition or validation.

But perhaps the most empowering aspect of my journey to building confidence has been the realisation that true strength lies in embracing vulnerability and authenticity. In a society that often prizes stoicism and emotional detachment, I learned to embrace my vulnerabilities and imperfections as sources of strength rather than weaknesses.

I allowed myself to be seen and heard, to speak my truth and stand firmly in my convictions, knowing that my authenticity is my greatest asset.

As I continue on my journey through life, I do so with a newfound sense of confidence and self-assurance. By embracing my true identity and individuality, despite the external pressures and expectations that seek to define me, I have discovered a sense of empowerment and freedom that transcends societal limitations and expectations. And as I navigate the complexities of today's society, I do so with the knowledge that my worth is not determined by the opinions or judgments of others, but by the love, acceptance, and respect I have for myself.

Key Takeaways:

- You're a limited-edition masterpiece - embrace your quirks and individuality!
- Your twenties are the "Quest for Self" chapter in your life's adventure book.
- Confidence is about being comfortable in your own skin, quirks and all.

Action Steps:

- Take a moment to celebrate one thing that makes you uniquely "you" today. Go ahead, give yourself a high-five!
- Try out a new hobby or activity that's been on your bucket list (even if it involves interpretive dance or learning the ancient art of cheese sculpting).
- Embrace a quirky trait or interest that you may have been shy about sharing with the world. Remember, being a bit weird is what makes life interesting!

ESSENTIAL LIFE TIPS FOR YOUR JOURNEY

- Reflect regularly – journaling, meditation, or even casual self-check-ins can help you understand your desires and fears.

- Step out of your comfort zone; growth often happens when you challenge yourself and try new experiences.

- Surround yourself with positive influences; relationships and environments that support your journey of self-discovery.

- Embrace failure as a lesson; each setback is an opportunity to learn more about yourself and your resilience.

- Define your own success; don't let societal expectations dictate your path. Create goals that resonate with your true self.

EMPOWERING AFFIRMATIONS

- I am on a journey of self-discovery, embracing my uniqueness and celebrating my authentic self.

- My past does not define me; every day is a chance to learn more about who I am and who I want to become.

- I trust my intuition and make choices that align with my values, creating a life that feels true to me.

- Self-love is my superpower; I radiate confidence and embrace every aspect of my evolving identity.

- I release the need for approval and embrace the freedom of being unapologetically myself.

SAY THESE OUT LOUD!

03

SETTING GOALS FOR A PURPOSEFUL FUTURE: TURNING DREAMS INTO REALITY

The Power of Goal Setting in Your Twenties

Alright, future world-changers let's have a heart-to-heart. Your twenties are like a canvas waiting for the masterpiece to be painted. But first, you need a brush, some colours, and a vision. That's where goals come in.

Think of them as the roadmap to your ultimate destination. Without them, you might end up in the middle of nowhere, singing sea shanties to the wind. And while that sounds fun, it's probably not the epic adventure you had in mind.

Creating a Vision for Your Personal and Professional Life

Close your eyes for a moment and imagine your ideal future. Are you in a corner office with a view? Exploring hidden gems in far-off lands? Or maybe you're the next viral sensation on TikTok?

Whatever it is, make it vivid. Taste it, feel it, and imagine the smell of success (or maybe just really good food if that's more your thing). This vision is your North Star, guiding you through the vast sea of possibilities.

Strategies for Achieving Milestones and Ambitions

Now, let's get tactical. Goals are like a giant jigsaw puzzle. You've got the big picture in your mind, but now it's time to break it down. Each piece represents a step, a milestone, a victory.

And guess what? Even if a piece doesn't fit right away, it's not the end of the world. You're not locked in a room with no exit. Life has more than one door, and it's perfectly fine to take a detour. Sometimes, those detours lead to the most unexpected and exciting discoveries.

Setting SMART Goals

In your twenties, setting SMART goals becomes pivotal in shaping your future with intention and purpose. Making goals Specific, Measurable, Achievable, Relevant, and Time-bound transforms dreams into actionable plans.

Firstly, ensure goals are Specific, defining precisely what you aim to achieve. Whether advancing in career, improving health, or acquiring new skills, clarity is key.

Next, make goals Measurable, with clear criteria to track progress. Whether monitoring savings, fitness, or professional development, tangible metrics keep you accountable and motivated.

Ensure goals are Achievable, setting realistic targets within reach. Dreaming big is commendable, yet setting achievable goals fosters a sense of accomplishment without overwhelm.

Ensure goals are Relevant to your vision and values. Ask, "Does this goal align with long-term aspirations? Does it contribute to personal growth?" Keeping goals relevant fosters focus and fulfilment.

Lastly, make goals Time-bound, setting deadlines to maintain accountability and motivation. Whether completing a project, reaching a fitness milestone, or achieving a financial target, deadlines in-still urgency and keep you on track.

By setting SMART goals in your twenties, you're not just envisioning your future—you're actively steering towards it, one goal at a time

Key Takeaways:

- Your twenties are your canvas; goals provide the brushstrokes for your masterpiece.
- Goals are your roadmap to prevent ending up in the middle of a sea shanty concert with no way home.
- Create a vivid vision of your future to serve as your guiding North Star.

Action Steps:

- Grab a notebook and jot down three big dreams for your twenties. Dreaming big is not only allowed but also encouraged!
- Choose one of those dreams and break it down into actionable steps. What's the first piece of your puzzle?
- Create a vision board or a digital collage to represent your goals. Surround yourself with reminders of the exciting journey ahead!

ESSENTIAL LIFE TIPS FOR YOUR JOURNEY

- Define clear and specific goals; the more precise, the easier it is to create actionable steps toward achievement

- Break big goals into smaller tasks; it makes the journey less overwhelming and more manageable.

- Stay flexible; be open to adjusting your goals as you grow and discover more about yourself.

- Visualise your success; create a vision board or mentally picture yourself achieving your goals to stay motivated.

- Surround yourself with a supportive community; share your goals with friends or mentors who can encourage and guide you.

EMPOWERING AFFIRMATIONS

- I am the architect of my destiny, setting ambitious goals that align with my passions and purpose.

- Every step I take towards my goals is a victory, and I celebrate my progress along the journey.

- I attract opportunities that propel me towards my goals, and I am open to the universe's abundance.

- My goals are a roadmap to my dreams; I break them down into achievable steps and tackle them with determination.

- I trust the timing of my life; even if things don't go as planned, I remain focused on my ultimate vision.

SAY THESE OUT LOUD!

CHAPTER

04

BUILDING RESILIENCE: THRIVING IN THE FACE OF TWENTIES' CHALLENGES

Understanding Resilience and Its Significance in Your Twenties

To my brave souls of the twenties, it's time to talk about resilience. Think of it as your life's greatest superpower - the ability to bounce back from setbacks like a champion. Your twenties are like a rollercoaster with a few unexpected loops and corkscrews. Resilience is the safety harness that keeps you secure.

Remember, even Batman had his bad days, but he always came back stronger. So, consider resilience in your Bat-suit for facing whatever Gotham - or life - throws your way.

Developing a Growth Mindset

Let's talk about mindset, shall we? A growth mindset is like a superhero cape for your brain. It's the belief that you can learn, adapt, and grow from any experience. So, when life throws lemons at you, not only do you make lemonade, but you also start a thriving lemonade empire.

A growth mindset means viewing challenges as opportunities for growth, not as obstacles. It's the difference between thinking, "I can't do this" and declaring, "Watch me conquer this!" So, when faced with a metaphorical supervillain, you'll confidently put on your metaphorical cape and save the day!

Embracing Change and Uncertainty
Your twenties are like a game of "Twister" - lots of limbs in the air, trying to find your balance. Embracing change is the secret to not toppling over. Sure, it's scary sometimes, but it's also where the magic happens.

So, when life decides to throw a plot twist your way, stand tall and say, "Is that all you got?" Because you've got resilience in your toolkit, and that's a game-changer.

My Personal Experience

The concept of a growth mindset has become a guiding principle in my journey through life. In today's society, where change is constant and challenges are plentiful, cultivating a growth mindset has been essential to my personal and professional development.

One of the most significant challenges I've faced was the decision to move to a new country. Leaving behind the familiar comforts of home and embarking on a journey into the unknown was both exhilarating and terrifying. Yet, I knew that growth often requires stepping outside of our comfort zones and embracing change with open arms.

Upon arriving in my new country, I was immediately confronted with a myriad of challenges. From navigating cultural differences to overcoming different barriers, every day seemed to present a new obstacle to overcome. But rather than allowing myself to be overwhelmed by fear or uncertainty, I chose to approach each challenge as an opportunity for growth and learning.

One of the key aspects of developing a growth mindset was reframing my perspective on failure. In a society that often equates failure with inadequacy or incompetence, I've learned to embrace failure as a natural part of the learning process. Every setback and mistake has become an opportunity for reflection and growth, pushing me to adapt and evolve in the face of adversity.

Furthermore, I've embraced the power of perseverance and determination in the pursuit of my goals. Whether it's mastering a new language, acclimating to a different work culture, or building a new social network, I refuse to be deterred by setbacks or obstacles along the way. Instead, I approach each challenge with a sense of optimism and tenacity, knowing that with hard work and dedication, anything is possible.

Another crucial aspect of developing a growth mindset has been the willingness to seek out new experiences and opportunities for personal growth. Whether it's enrolling in language classes, volunteering in my community, or immersing myself in the local culture, I've embraced every opportunity to expand my horizons and broaden my perspective. By embracing change and stepping outside of my comfort zone, I've discovered new passions, developed new skills, and forged meaningful connections with others.

But perhaps the most transformative aspect of my journey to developing a growth mindset has been the realisation that growth is not a destination, but a continuous journey. In today's fast-paced society, where change is constant and the only constant is uncertainty, I've learned to embrace the unknown with open arms, knowing that every challenge and obstacle is an opportunity for growth and self-discovery.

As I continue on my journey through life, I do so with a sense of optimism and excitement for the future. By cultivating a growth mindset and embracing change with open arms, I know that I have the power to overcome any challenge that comes my way and achieve my dreams. And as I look back on my journey thus far, I do so with a deep sense of gratitude for the opportunities for growth and transformation that have come my way.

Key Takeaways:
- Resilience is your secret weapon, allowing you to bounce back from setbacks stronger than before.
- A growth mindset is your ticket to soaring through challenges and turning them into opportunities for greatness. The belief is that you can learn, adapt, and grow from any experience.
- Embracing change is where the magic happens; it's your secret to staying balanced in the whirlwind of your twenties.

Action Steps:
- Reflect on a past challenge you faced and how you overcame it. Celebrate your own resilience!
- Choose one area in your life where you'd like to adopt a growth mindset. How can you approach challenges with a newfound sense of opportunity?
- Embrace a small change in your routine or environment this week. It could be as simple as trying a new hobby or taking a different route to work. Remember, it's all part of the adventure!

ESSENTIAL LIFE TIPS FOR YOUR JOURNEY

- Cultivate a growth mindset; see challenges as opportunities to learn and develop new skills.

- Build a strong support system; surround yourself with friends and mentors who uplift and inspire you.

- Practice self-compassion; treat yourself with kindness during difficult times and acknowledge your efforts.

- Break challenges into smaller tasks; it's easier to overcome obstacles when you take them one step at a time.

- Celebrate small victories; recognising progress, no matter how small, boosts your confidence and resilience.

- I bounce back from challenges stronger than before, turning setbacks into stepping stones for success.

- Resilience is my superpower; I embrace difficulties as opportunities to grow and learn.

- I trust in my ability to navigate life's twists and turns, knowing that every challenge is temporary.

- I am not defined by tough times; I define them by my unwavering strength and resilience.

- Adversity is a chance to showcase my resilience, and I face it with courage and a positive mindset.

SAY THESE OUT LOUD!

CHAPTER

05

NAVIGATING RELATIONSHIPS: BUILDING MEANINGFUL CONNECTIONS

Cultivating Healthy Friendships and Romantic Relationships

Let's talk about the cast of characters in your life's story. Think of them as the members of your own Dream Team – each with their unique strengths and quirks, ready to face challenges and celebrate victories alongside you.

But here's the thing: Quality trumps quantity. It's better to have a handful of true allies than a legion of fair-weather friends. So, seek out those who not only stand with you in the sunshine but dance with you in the rain.

Effective Communication and Active Listening Skills

Communication is your beacon in the fog. It's how you send out signals for help, share your triumphs, and make sense of the world. However, remember that being a good communicator isn't just about broadcasting your message; it's about tuning in to the signals around you.

Imagine trying to conduct an orchestra without listening to the musicians! It's the harmony of both speaking and listening that creates beautiful music in your relationships. So, put away distractions and truly hear what your companions are saying. It's not just about sharing; it's about truly connecting.

Setting Boundaries for Positive Interactions

Boundaries are your sanctuary, a space where you can be your true self without fear of intrusion. Whether it's declining an invitation to a social event or redirecting a conversation that's heading into uncomfortable territory, don't be afraid to establish boundaries.

Your boundaries are like the walls of your castle, protecting your well-being and ensuring that your relationships flourish in an atmosphere of respect and understanding.

My Personal Experience

As I reflect on my own journey through this rollercoaster of emotions, connections, and growth, I can't help but smile at the memories, lessons, and the beautiful chaos that comes with it.

In our early twenties, friendships become the backbone of our social existence. The transition from the safety net of high school cliques to the vast expanse of adulthood is both exhilarating and intimidating. The first few years often feel like a crash course in social dynamics, where you meet a vast amount of personalities, each contributing to the mosaic of your life.

In my case, I was blessed with a tight-knit group of friends from college who embarked on this journey alongside me. We were a very diverse and multicultural group, each bringing something unique to the table. Together, we dealt with the challenges of entering the workforce in a new country, chasing our dreams, and just trying to make a living on our own.

Friendships, however, are not immune to change. As we embraced our individual paths, our group shifted. New friendships were forged, and some old ones faced the test of time. It was during this period that I discovered the importance of evolving with friendship.

One of the most defining moments occurred when I decided to relocate for a job opportunity to another country. Initially, I felt sad, fearing that distance might ruin the bonds we had built over late-night study sessions and spontaneous road trips.However, these were friendships I had that developed from college that became family, so I didn't need to worry.

Technology became our bridge. Late-night calls replaced impromptu hangouts, and video chats turned into virtual reunions. In this era of constant connectivity, I realised that maintaining friendships isn't solely dependent on physical proximity but rather on the effort invested in staying connected. It was a valuable lesson in adapting to change and cherishing the essence of friendship beyond its physical manifestations.

As friendships underwent transformations, romantic relationships also played a significant role in shaping my twenties. Trying to understand love and to feel loved brought its fair share of highs and lows, teaching me invaluable lessons about vulnerability, communication, and self-discovery.

I found myself in entanglements searching to find what it meant to be loved. The early twenties were an eye opener that real life romance is nothing like the romance films I used to watch or novels I used to read. Along came Mr. Knight in shining armour who stuck with me throughout my early twenties. I fell in love and I fell hard, however, the flames that burn the brightest often burn out the quickest.

The aftermath of that intense affair left me grappling with heartbreak and a profound sense of loss. Yet, within that darkness, I discovered the resilience of the human spirit. The journey to healing became an exploration of self-love, understanding the importance of being whole independently before seeking completeness in someone else.

In the wake of heartache, I found solace in friendships. Friends became the pillars of support, offering a safe space to vent, reflect, and eventually heal. It was during this period that I understood that having the right people around you can create a huge positive impact in your life. Relationships might bring passion and intimacy, however, true friendship provides stability and unconditional support.

After healing and feeling brand new, I approached romantic relationships with newfound wisdom. The following connections were marked by a deeper understanding of myself and my needs. I learned to communicate openly, set boundaries, and appreciate the beauty of two individuals coexisting without losing their individual essence.

In the mid-twenties, the landscape of friendships and relationships expanded further as career aspirations took centre stage. Balancing professional ambitions with personal connections became a challenge. The challenge was not just in finding time but in prioritising and nurturing the relationships that truly mattered.

During this pursuit, I discovered that quality triumphs over quantity when it comes to friendships. I found myself investing energy in relationships that added value to my life. The art of saying 'no' to toxic relationships and 'yes' to those that foster growth.

At my workplace, I realised building meaningful professional relationships involves mutual respect, shared goals, and a genuine interest in each other's success. Navigating office dynamics taught me the importance of cultivating relationships with colleagues and mentors. These connections not only contribute to personal growth but also open doors to many amazing opportunities. In your twenties, the ability to build a network is as crucial as the skills listed on a resume.

As the twenties draw to a close, and the threshold of the thirties is right around the corner, I find myself standing at the intersection of nostalgia and anticipation. The friendships that weathered the storms, the romantic entanglements that shaped my understanding of love, and the professional connections that paved the way for future endeavours – each are a significant part of how I thrive in my twenties as they hold a story worth cherishing.

Key Takeaways:

- Your social circle is your very own Dream Team – choose companions who are ready to stand with you in both sunshine and rain.
- Communication is your beacon in the fog, and it's a two-way street. Active listening is the cornerstone of meaningful connections.
- Boundaries create a sanctuary for authentic interaction, ensuring that your relationships flourish in an atmosphere of respect and understanding.

Action Steps:

- Reflect on your current social circle. Identify the allies who consistently support and uplift you and consider if there are any relationships in your life that may need a bit of re-evaluation.
- Practice active listening in your next interaction. Put away distractions and focus on truly hearing what the other person is conveying. Watch how it deepens your connection.
- Identify one area where you'd like to establish or reinforce boundaries in your relationships. It could be a specific situation or a general practice of self-care. Remember, your sanctuary, your rules!

ESSENTIAL LIFE TIPS FOR YOUR JOURNEY

- Be present in conversations; put away distractions and give your full attention to the person you're with.

- Show vulnerability; sharing your true self helps build trust and creates deeper connections.

- Set boundaries; communicate your needs and ensure that relationships are mutually respectful and supportive.

- Invest time in building diverse connections; different perspectives enrich your life and broaden your horizons.

- Practice empathy; understanding others' perspectives fosters stronger, more meaningful relationships.

EMPOWERING AFFIRMATIONS

- I attract positive and genuine connections into my life, nurturing relationships that align with my values.

- Every interaction is an opportunity to build a meaningful connection, and I approach them with authenticity and openness.

- I value my own company and choose relationships that add joy and fulfilment to my life.

- I communicate openly and actively listen, fostering deep connections that go beyond surface-level interactions.

- I trust the timing of relationships; the right people come into my life at the right moments.

SAY THESE OUT LOUD!

06

MASTERING TIME MANAGEMENT: BALANCING WORK, LIFE, AND AMBITIONS

Prioritising and Organising Your Time in Your Twenties

Let's step into the grand arena of time management. Your twenties are like a bustling carnival, filled with attractions of work, personal pursuits, and ambitions. But fear not! With a pinch of strategy and a sprinkle of wit, you'll become the ringmaster of your own time.

Time-Blocking and Task Prioritisation Techniques

Imagine your day as a symphony. Each task is an instrument, contributing to the harmonious melody of productivity. Time-blocking is your conductor's baton, ensuring that each instrument plays its part at the right moment. It's not about controlling time; it's about orchestrating it to create a masterpiece.

And let's not forget about prioritisation. It's like handing out golden tickets to the most important tasks. Don't waste them on sideshows; reserve them for the main event.

Creating Effective Schedules for Productivity

Your day is your canvas, and a well-crafted schedule is the brush that paints your masterpiece. Start with broad strokes - allocate time for work, personal pursuits, and rest. Then, add finer details - specific tasks, meetings, and moments for self-care.

But here's the twist: leave room for spontaneity. Every masterpiece needs a touch of playfulness, a hidden gem of unexpected joy.

Maximising Efficiency and Focus

Now, let's talk about goals. They're like the treasure chests hidden within your day, waiting to be discovered. To find them, you'll need a map - a clear vision of what you want to achieve. Once you have it, channel your inner explorer and set off on your quest.

Efficiency and focus are your trusty companions on this journey. They'll help you navigate distractions, dodge detours, and stay on course towards your treasure trove of accomplishments.

Balancing Career Aspirations, Personal Life, and Pursuits

Managing your career, personal life, and aspirations is akin to balancing multiple apps on your smartphone. Each one demands attention, yet a harmonious integration results in a fulfilling user experience. Strive for a seamless synergy where work, personal life, and dreams complement one another without overwhelming your mental bandwidth.

Consider those brief moments of screen downtime as opportunities for mindfulness and self-renewal in our fast-paced digital landscape.

My Personal Experience

In the whirlwind of modern life, mastering time management can feel like chasing a unicorn—elusive and mythical. As a 28-year-old woman navigating the maze of responsibilities, ambitions, and desires, I found myself teetering on the edge of chaos. Balancing work, personal life, and aspirations seemed akin to juggling flaming torches. Yet, in the midst of this chaos, I discovered the art of harmonising my time, a journey that transformed my life.

I must admit, the journey wasn't without its trials and tribulations. Like many young professionals, I found myself caught in the relentless grip of work obligations. Deadlines loomed ominously, meetings stretched into infinity, and emails flooded my inbox like an unstoppable tide. The pressure was suffocating, threatening to consume every waking moment of my existence, so draining.

Amidst this chaos, I realised that time was a precious commodity, one that I couldn't afford to squander. It was then that I embarked on a quest to reclaim control over my schedule and, ultimately, my life.

The first step was acknowledging the power of prioritization. I learned to distinguish between tasks that were urgent and those that were merely important. By allocating my time according to the Eisenhower Matrix—sorting tasks into four categories: urgent and important, important but not urgent, urgent but not important, and neither urgent nor important—I was able to focus my energy on activities that truly mattered.

Furthermore, I embraced the concept of batching similar tasks together. Rather than flitting from one task to another like a frenzied hummingbird, I consolidated similar activities into dedicated time blocks. This not only minimized distractions but also maximized efficiency, allowing me to accomplish more in less time.

Of course, no discussion of time management would be complete without addressing the elephant in the room: procrastination. Ah, Procrastination, beckoning me with its sweet promises of momentary respite. But I refused to succumb to its allure. Instead, I employed various strategies to combat procrastination, from breaking tasks down into smaller, more manageable chunks to utilizing time-blocking techniques to create a sense of urgency.

Yet, amidst the hustle and bustle of professional life, I refused to neglect my personal well-being. Self-care became my mantra, a guiding principle that infused every aspect of my life. Whether it was indulging in a leisurely bubble bath, immersing myself in a good book, or simply taking a leisurely stroll through the park, I made a conscious effort to prioritise self-care, recognising that a healthy mind and body were the cornerstones of productivity.

The most transformative aspect of my journey was the realisation that time management wasn't merely about checking items off a to-do list—it was about aligning my actions with my values and aspirations. I took the time to reflect on my long-term goals, crafting a roadmap that would guide me towards the life I envisioned for myself.

In doing so, I discovered a newfound sense of purpose and direction, one that propelled me forward with unwavering determination. Armed with a newfound sense of clarity, I embarked on a journey of self-discovery and personal growth, unearthing hidden talents and passions along the way.

Today, as I reflect on my journey to mastering time management as a young adult, I am filled with a profound sense of gratitude. Gratitude for the lessons learned, the challenging obstacles (social media) overcome, and the person I have become as a result. I discovered not only the power to shape my destiny but also became resilient. And for that, I am eternally grateful.

Key Takeaways:

- Time management is your gateway to becoming the ringmaster of your own carnival of tasks and ambitions.
- Time-blocking and prioritisation techniques help orchestrate your day for maximum productivity and goal achievement.
- Crafting effective schedules allows you to paint a daily masterpiece, balancing work, personal pursuits, and rest.

Action Steps:

- Experiment with time-blocking. Allocate specific time slots for tasks and observe how it enhances your productivity.
- Craft a daily schedule that balances work, personal pursuits, and self-care. Leave room for spontaneity and unexpected joys.
- Define a clear goal for the week. Use efficiency and focus to navigate towards its accomplishment, like a treasure hunt for success.
- Reflect on moments of balance in your life. Identify areas where work, personal life, and ambitions complement and harmonise with each other.

ESSENTIAL LIFE TIPS FOR YOUR JOURNEY

- Use productivity tools wisely; apps and planners are your allies in managing tasks and deadlines.

- Prioritise tasks based on urgency and importance, ensuring you tackle what truly matters first.

- Set realistic goals; breaking them down into smaller, achievable steps helps manage your time effectively.

- Practice the 2-minute rule; if a task takes less than 2 minutes, do it immediately to avoid piling up.

- Schedule downtime; plan breaks and leisure activities to recharge and maintain a healthy work-life balance.

EMPOWERING AFFIRMATIONS

- I am the master of my time, balancing work, life, and my ambitions with grace and efficiency.

- Each moment is an opportunity, and I use my time wisely to pursue my passions and achieve my goals.

- I prioritise self-care, recognising that a well-rested and fulfilled me is crucial for success.

- My schedule reflects my values, and I allocate time to what truly matters in both my personal and professional life.

- I am in control of my time, avoiding procrastination and making progress toward my dreams every day.

SAY THESE OUT LOUD!

CHAPTER

07

PRIORITISING YOUR WELL-BEING: NURTURING MENTAL AND PHYSICAL HEALTH

Understanding the Importance of Self-Care in Your Twenties

It's time for a heart-to-heart about self-care. Think of it as your own anthem, a serenade to your well-being. In this bustling decade, it's easy to get caught up in the whirlwind but remember, self-care isn't selfish; it's the foundation for a thriving, balanced life.

Recognising that you deserve care and attention is the first step to nurturing your mental and physical health. So, let's embark on this journey of self-discovery and growth, with self-care as our guiding melody.

Recognising and Addressing Mental Health Needs

Your mental health is like a delicate musical instrument, requiring tune-ups and care. It's okay to acknowledge when the strings are out of tune. Recognising and addressing mental health needs is an act of strength, not weakness.

Imagine it's a garden – tend to it with mindfulness, water it with self-compassion, and let the sun of self-reflection shine on it. Seek support when needed, and remember, you're not alone in this symphony.

Incorporating Physical Wellness into Daily Life

Picture physical wellness as a graceful waltz, a dance of movement and vitality. It's not about gruelling marathons; it's about finding joy in motion. Incorporate activities that you enjoy, whether it's a morning yoga routine or an evening dance class.

Remember, movement is a celebration of what your body can do, not a punishment for what it looks like. So, put on your dancing shoes and let physical wellness be your partner in this beautiful waltz of life.

Remember, movement is a celebration of what your body can do, not a punishment for what it looks like. So, put on your dancing shoes and let physical wellness be your partner in this beautiful waltz of life.

Healthful Habits: Nutrition, Exercise, and Sleep Hygiene Tips

Let's talk about the trio of healthful habits: nutrition, exercise, and sleep. Think of them as the three supporting pillars of your well-being temple. Nourish your body with wholesome foods, move it with activities that bring you joy, and rest it with the care it deserves.

But here's a secret: it's not about perfection, but progress. Small, sustainable changes can lead to lasting transformations. So, savour each step on this journey of healthful living.

SLEEP HYGIENE TIPS

Stick to a Routine: Make friends with a consistent sleep schedule. Your body loves predictability, so aim to hit the hay and rise at the same time daily.

Chill Vibes Only: Wind down with a cosy bedtime routine. Whether it's a good book, soothing tunes, or a warm bath – find what chills you out before hitting the pillow.

Tech Break Before Bed: Let your devices snooze before you do. The blue light messes with your sleep vibes, so give yourself at least 30 minutes of tech-free time before bedtime.

Caffeine Curfew: Watch the caffeine intake, especially in the afternoon. Swap that late-day coffee for some herbal tea or decaf goodness to avoid turning bedtime into a staring contest with the ceiling.

Move That Body: Get your groove on with regular exercise. It's like a secret weapon for better sleep. Just try to finish your workout a few hours before bedtime so your body has time to cool down.

My Personal Experience

In today's fast-paced society, the pursuit of physical and mental well-being can feel like an uphill battle. Navigating the maze of modern life, I've learned firsthand the importance of prioritising self-care amidst the chaos. Balancing work, social obligations, and personal aspirations often leaves little room for nurturing my physical and mental health, but I've discovered that carving out space for self-care is not just a luxury—it's a necessity.

One of the key pillars of my journey towards optimal health has been establishing a consistent exercise routine. Incorporating physical activity into my daily life has not only improved my physical fitness but has also been instrumental in managing stress and boosting my mood. Whether it's hitting the gym for a heart-pumping workout, going for a run in the park, or practicing yoga in the comfort of my own home, exercise has become my sanctuary—a sacred space where I can escape the pressures of daily life and reconnect with myself.

In addition to prioritizing physical activity, I've also made a conscious effort to nourish my body with wholesome, nutritious food. As a Caribbean woman, I recognise the importance of honouring my cultural heritage through the foods I eat, incorporating traditional dishes and ingredients that not only satisfy my taste buds but also nourish my body from the inside out. From Caribbean stews and spices to vibrant salads and delicious fruits, I've embraced a diverse array of flavours and textures that not only fuel my body but also feed my soul.

But nurturing my physical health is only part of the equation—I've also prioritized my mental well-being with equal fervor. In a society that often stigmatizes mental health issues, I've made it a point to prioritize self-awareness and emotional resilience. This means carving out time for activities that bring me joy and fulfillment, whether it's indulging in creative hobbies like painting or writing, spending quality time with loved ones, or simply taking a moment to pause and breathe amidst the chaos of daily life.

Furthermore, I've cultivated a strong support network of friends, family, and mental health professionals who provide me with the love, encouragement, and guidance I need to navigate life's challenges with grace and resilience.

Whether it's seeking therapy to work through past traumas and anxieties, participating in support groups to connect with others who share similar experiences, or simply reaching out to a trusted friend for a listening ear, I've learned that asking for help is not a sign of weakness but a testament to my strength and resilience.

In today's society, where the pressures of work, social media, and societal expectations can feel overwhelming, nurturing both my physical and mental health has become a non-negotiable priority. By prioritising self-care, I've not only improved my overall quality of life but have also cultivated a deep sense of self-love and acceptance that empowers me to navigate life's challenges with courage and grace.

Key Takeaways:

- Self-care is your personal anthem, the foundation for a thriving, balanced life in your twenties.
- Recognising and addressing mental health needs is an act of strength, like tending to a delicate musical instrument or a garden in need of care.
- Physical wellness is a graceful waltz, a celebration of movement and vitality that brings joy and vitality to your life.

Action Steps:

- Reflect on one self-care practice that resonates with you. How can you incorporate it into your routine this week?
- Identify a mental health resource or support system you can turn to if needed. Remember, seeking help is a sign of strength and courage.
- Choose one physical activity that brings you joy. Plan to integrate it into your schedule regularly, turning it into a delightful dance of wellness.
- Make a small, healthful change in your nutrition, exercise, or sleep routine. It could be trying a new recipe, starting a morning stretching routine, or setting a bedtime routine for better sleep.

ESSENTIAL LIFE TIPS FOR YOUR JOURNEY

- Make exercise a daily joy; find physical activities that you genuinely enjoy, making exercise a pleasure, not a chore.

- Prioritise quality sleep; a well-rested mind and body are your greatest assets for navigating life's challenges.

- Nourish your body with whole foods that fuel your energy and support your overall health.

- Practice mindfulness; take moments to breathe deeply, centre yourself, and appreciate the present.

- Cultivate a positive environment; surround yourself with people and experiences that uplift your spirits.

EMPOWERING AFFIRMATIONS

- My well-being is my top priority; I honor my body and mind with choices that nurture both.

- I embrace self-care as a non-negotiable part of my routine, understanding its impact on my overall happiness.

- Every healthy choice I make is an investment in my long-term well-being, and I am worth that investment.

- I listen to my body and mind, giving them the rest they need to function at their best.

- I release stress and negativity, creating space for positive energy and well-being to thrive.

SAY THESE OUT LOUD!

CHAPTER

08

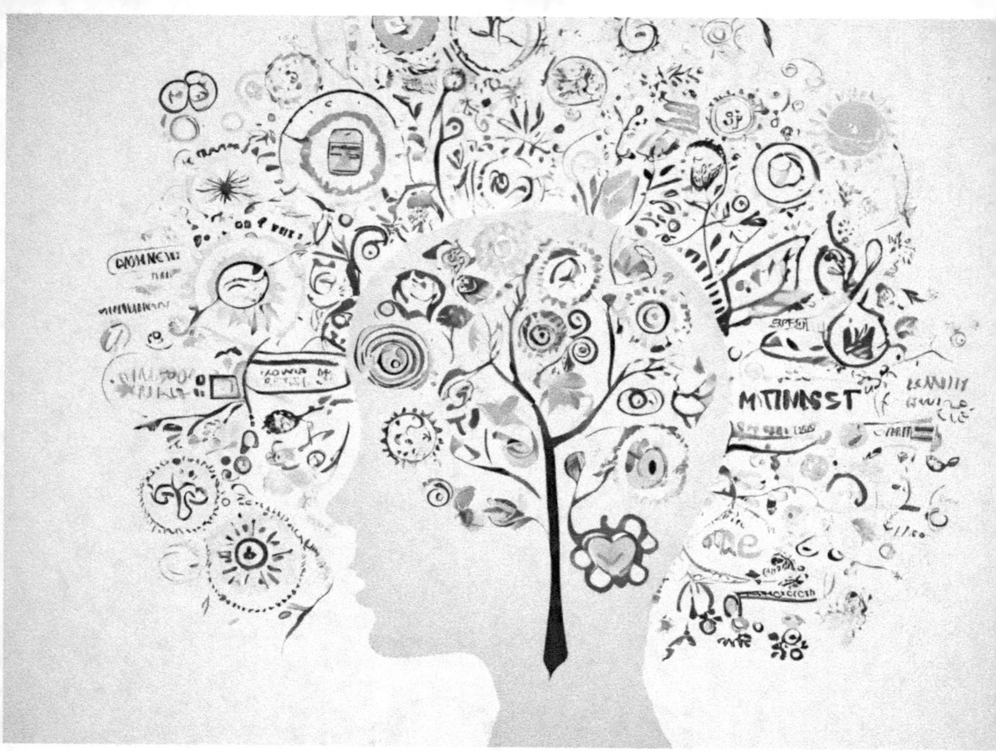

EMPOWERING YOUR MINDSET: CULTIVATING POSITIVITY AND GROWTH

Harnessing the Power of a Positive Mindset for Success

Let's embark on a mindset makeover adventure. Think of it like upgrading your mental software - you know, giving your brain a cool new interface with all the latest features. After all, we're in our twenties; it's time for an upgrade, isn't it?

Remember, a positive mindset is like Wi-Fi for your soul - you might not see it, but it's there, making things work and helping you stay connected to your dreams and goals.

Cultivating Optimism and Positivity in Daily Life

Imagine your brain as a playlist, and positive thoughts are like your favourite jams. They're there to boost your mood, even on days when your inner DJ is feeling a bit moody. Like that one song that always gets you dancing, positive thoughts can turn even the gloomiest day into a little dance party in your head.

And guess what? The more you play these upbeat tunes, the more you'll find yourself dancing through life's challenges.

Recognising and Challenging Negative Thought Patterns

Let's face it, our brains sometimes throw a little temper tantrum. Negative thought patterns can be like that one friend who insists on playing the same sad song on repeat. But here's the thing: you have the remote control, and you can always change the channel.

Imagine your mind as a meme generator, constantly churning out thoughts that make you smile, laugh, and feel empowered. Negative thoughts might try to sneak in, but you've got a treasure chest of positivity memes ready to take centre stage!

Resilient Roots: Gratitude, Optimism, and Resilience

Gratitude, optimism, and resilience are some of the power trios of your twenties. They're the squad that shows up when life throws unexpected curveballs.

Gratitude is like your personal hype person, reminding you to celebrate even the tiniest victories, like finally conquering that tricky recipe.

Optimism is your motivational coach, pushing you to chase your dreams, even if they seem a little wild.

And resilience? Well, that's your secret weapon, helping you bounce back from rejections, setbacks, and the occasional mismatched sock crisis!

My Personal Experience

Maintaining a positive mindset in today's society has been both a challenge and a triumph. In a world that often seems intent on stacking the odds against me, I've learned to, find strength and solace in the face of adversity.

From the moment I entered adulthood, I quickly became aware of the myriad challenges that Black women face on a daily basis. Whether it's systemic racism, gender discrimination, or societal expectations, the road ahead often feels fraught with obstacles. But rather than allowing myself to be consumed by bitterness or despair, I've chosen to approach life with an unwavering optimism and a steadfast belief in my own worth.

One of the key strategies I've leaned on to maintain a positive mindset is the practice of self-love and self-acceptance. In a society that often seeks to diminish our worth and undermine our confidence, I've made it a point to celebrate my uniqueness and embrace my identity as a Black woman.

I refuse to conform to narrow beauty standards or internalise harmful stereotypes. Instead, I celebrate my beauty, intelligence, and resilience, recognising that they are sources of strength rather than limitations.

Furthermore, I've surrounded myself with a supportive community of friends, family, and mentors who uplift and empower me on my journey. Whether it's sharing laughs over brunch, lending a listening ear during times of struggle, or offering words of encouragement and wisdom, these relationships have been instrumental in helping me navigate the ups and downs of life with grace and dignity.

In addition to cultivating a strong support network, I've also prioritised my mental health and well-being. In a society that often stigmatises mental illness and denies us access to quality healthcare, I've made it a point to prioritise self-care and seek out resources that promote mental wellness. Whether it's practicing mindfulness and meditation, seeking therapy to process past traumas and challenges, or engaging in activities that bring me joy and fulfilment, I refuse to let the weight of the world crush my spirit. Instead, I choose to nurture my mind, body, and soul, recognising that self-care is not selfish but essential to my survival and thriving.

But perhaps the most important lesson I've learned on my journey to maintaining a positive mindset is the power of resilience. Despite the countless obstacles and setbacks I've encountered along the way, I refuse to be defined by my circumstances or limited by the expectations of others. Instead, I embrace every challenge as an opportunity for growth and transformation, knowing that with perseverance and determination, I can overcome any obstacle that stands in my way.

In today's world, where the odds often seem stacked against us, maintaining a positive mindset as a Black young adult in her twenties is no easy feat. But through self-love, community support, prioritising mental health, and cultivating resilience, I've learned to navigate life's challenges with unwavering optimism. As I continue on this journey, I do so with the knowledge that my strength, resilience, and positivity are not just survival mechanisms—they are the keys to unlocking a future filled with boundless opportunities and endless possibilities.

Key Takeaways:

- A positive mindset is like having a supercharged app for life – it's there to help you navigate the ups and downs of your twenties with style.
- Cultivating optimism is like having a trusty sidekick who reminds you that even on rough days, there's always a silver lining.
- Remember, you're the chief editor of your mental newspaper – let in the stories that inspire, motivate, and make you laugh out loud!

Action Steps:

- Start a gratitude journal. Jot down three things you're thankful for each day, whether it's your morning coffee, a funny meme, or a heartwarming text from a friend.
- Give your negative thought patterns quirky names. The next time they pop up, imagine them wearing funny costumes or speaking in a silly voice.
- Embrace setbacks with the determination of a pizza delivery person finding your apartment in a mazy building. Remember, you have the power to find your way!

ESSENTIAL LIFE TIPS FOR YOUR JOURNEY

- Start your day with gratitude; acknowledging the positive aspects of your life sets a tone for positivity.

- Challenge negative thoughts; replace them with affirmations that empower and uplift your mindset.

- Learn from criticism; view it as constructive feedback that contributes to your personal and professional growth.

- Cultivate a learning mindset; see every experience as an opportunity to gain knowledge and develop new skills.

- Surround yourself with positivity; engage in activities, relationships, and environments that foster growth and optimism.

EMPOWERING AFFIRMATIONS

- I am the creator of my reality, and I choose to cultivate a mindset that attracts positivity and growth.

- Challenges are opportunities in disguise, and I face them with resilience, knowing they lead to personal evolution.

- I celebrate my progress, big or small, recognising that growth is a continuous journey, not a destination.

- My mindset shapes my experiences; I choose optimism and believe in the power of my potential.

- Every setback is a setup for a comeback; I embrace setbacks as stepping stones toward success.

SAY THESE OUT LOUD!

CHAPTER

09

FINANCIAL LITERACY: BUILDING A FOUNDATION FOR FINANCIAL INDEPENDENCE

Budgeting and Financial Planning for Twenties

Think of your budget as your trusty sidekick, equipped with the power to turn your financial dreams into reality.

Budgeting isn't about being a money Scrooge, it's about being a wise financial wizard, ensuring that every dollar finds its perfect place in your financial kingdom.

Creating and Managing a Budget for Financial Stability

Imagine your budget as a treasure map, leading you to the financial X that marks the spot of stability and security. But don't worry, there are no hidden traps or riddles – just a bit of thoughtful planning.

Start by giving your budget a fun name, like "Operation Financial Freedom." This way, you're not just managing money, you're on a daring mission!

Setting Financial Goals and Priorities

Let's talk about goals. Picture them as stamps in your passport to financial adventures. Each stamp represents a milestone – whether it's the "Homeowner" stamp or the "World Traveler" stamp.

But remember, you don't have to collect them all at once. Prioritise your goals based on what excites you the most right now. It's like choosing which ride to go on first at the financial theme park!

Saving, Investing, and Managing Debt

Saving is like training for a marathon - it's a bit of a challenge, but the feeling of accomplishment is absolutely worth it. Start by setting up an automatic transfer to your savings account, treating it like a monthly subscription to your future dreams.

Investing is like joining a financial gym - it might feel intimidating at first, but with the right guidance, you'll be flexing those financial muscles in no time.

Debt management is like playing a game of "Debt Jenga." With each smart move, you're carefully removing blocks without toppling the tower of your financial stability. It's all about finding that delicate balance!

Investments are like seeds you plant in a magical money garden. With a bit of care and patience, they'll grow into a forest of financial security.

Long-term planning is like being the director of your own financial blockbuster. You're calling the shots, setting the scenes, and ensuring a happy ending where you retire on your own terms!

My Personal Experience

Managing my finances has been a journey filled with challenges, triumphs, and everything in between. With the ever-rising cost of living and the impending danger of economic uncertainty, budgeting and saving for the future have become essential components of my everyday life.

From the moment I entered the workforce, I quickly realized the importance of creating a budget to effectively manage my finances. With a steady income but a plethora of expenses, including rent, utilities, groceries, transportation, and loan payments, I knew that every dollar had to be accounted for. So, armed with a spreadsheet and a determination to take control of my financial destiny, I dove headfirst into the world of budgeting.

Creating a budget was the easy part—sticking to it proved to be the real challenge. With so many temptations and unexpected expenses lurking around every corner, it often felt like I was walking a tightrope, teetering on the edge of financial instability. But through discipline, determination, and a healthy dose of trial and error, I gradually learned to make smart financial decisions that aligned with my long-term goals.

One of the biggest hurdles I faced was learning to distinguish between wants and needs. In a society that bombards us with messages of consumerism and instant gratification, it's all too easy to succumb to the allure of impulse purchases and frivolous spending. But I quickly realised that true financial freedom lay not in the latest gadgets or designer handbags, but in the ability to live within my means and prioritise my financial future.

To that end, I adopted a minimalist mindset, decluttering my life of unnecessary possessions and reevaluating my spending habits. I became a master of meal prepping, opting for home cooked meals over expensive takeout, and embraced the joy of thrifting, scouring thrift stores for hidden treasures. Every penny saved brought me one step closer to my financial goals, whether it was building an emergency fund, paying off debt, or saving for retirement.

Of course, navigating the current economic climate hasn't been without its fair share of obstacles. With the cost of living skyrocketing and wages stagnating, it often feels like I'm fighting an uphill battle. But rather than succumbing to despair, I've chosen to focus on what I can control—namely, my own spending habits and financial priorities.

In times of uncertainty, I've learned to be adaptable and resourceful, seeking out creative solutions to stretch my dollars further. Whether it's negotiating lower bills, taking advantage of coupons and discounts, or exploring alternative income streams like freelance work or side hustles, I've refused to let economic adversity dictate my financial future.

Despite the challenges and setbacks I've encountered along the way, I remain hopeful and optimistic about what the future holds. By embracing the principles of budgeting, saving, and financial independence, I've laid the foundation for a brighter tomorrow—one where I can live life on my own terms, free from the shackles of financial insecurity. And as I continue on this journey, I take comfort in knowing that every dollar saved brings me one step closer to the life of abundance and prosperity that I deserve.

Key Takeaways:

- Budgeting is key to helping you turn your financial dreams into reality, one dollar at a time.
- Setting financial goals is like choosing your own adventure – prioritise based on what excites you the most right now.
- Saving, investing, and debt management are the tools in your financial toolkit, helping you build a solid foundation for your future.

Action Steps:

- Give your budget a fun name or theme. Share it with a friend and make it a friendly competition to see who can save more!
- Create a vision board with images representing your top financial goals. Display it where you'll see it daily for an extra dose of motivation.
- Join a financial literacy group or online community to exchange tips and celebrate small victories along your financial journey.

ESSENTIAL LIFE TIPS FOR YOUR JOURNEY

- Create a budget that aligns with your goals; knowing where your money goes is the first step to financial empowerment.

- Save consistently; even small amounts add up over time, creating a safety net for the future.

- Invest in your financial education; understanding money management and investment basics is crucial for long-term success.

- Live below your means; finding joy in simplicity allows you to save and invest more for your future self.

- Set financial goals; having clear objectives motivates you to make informed decisions and stay on track.

EMPOWERING AFFIRMATIONS

- I am in control of my finances, making mindful decisions that lead me toward financial independence.

- Every dollar I save is a step towards financial freedom, and I celebrate my smart money moves.

- I am building a strong financial foundation, creating opportunities for future success and security.

- Money is a tool, and I use it wisely to create the life I desire and achieve my financial goals.

- I am grateful for my financial journey, learning and growing as I move towards independence.

SAY THESE OUT LOUD!

10

CRAFTING YOUR FUTURE: MAKING INFORMED DECISIONS FOR A FULFILLING LIFE

Defining Your Values and Aspirations for Your Twenties and Beyond

It's time to embark on a grand vision quest. Think of it as a treasure hunt for your core values, those guiding principles that light the way through life's twists and turns.

Consider this: if life were a buffet, what values would you heap on your plate?

Is it a heaping scoop of creativity, a sprinkle of adventure, or a generous serving of kindness?

Reflecting on Personal Values and Beliefs

Imagine a magical mirror that doesn't reflect your image, but instead projects your values and beliefs in bright, neon colours. Take a moment to stand before it. What does it reveal? Perhaps it illuminates your passion for justice or your unwavering belief in kindness.

Now, picture yourself stepping through that mirror, embodying those values in every decision you make. It's like wearing a cloak of authenticity wherever you go.

Aligning Goals with Your Core Values

Setting goals isn't just about scribbling wishes on a piece of paper - it's about weaving the fabric of your future. Picture your goals as threads, each one contributing to the rich tapestry of your life.

For instance, if "connection" is a core value, consider setting a goal to deepen your relationships or seek out opportunities for meaningful collaborations. That way, every step forward is a step towards a more authentic and fulfilling life.

Now, let's roll up our sleeves and get to work. Crafting your future is like sculpting a masterpiece. You have the raw materials – your values, beliefs, and goals. It's time to chisel away at the excess, revealing the beautiful, authentic you.

Remember, even Michelangelo had to weather a few chisel slips. Embrace the imperfections and keep carving. You're sculpting a future that's uniquely yours.

My Personal Experience

One of the most empowering aspects of this journey has been learning to make informed decisions for my future, aligning my goals with my core values and beliefs to create a life that reflects who I am and what I stand for.

Central to my approach to decision-making has been the process of introspection and self-reflection. By taking the time to explore my values, beliefs, and aspirations, I've gained clarity and insight into what truly matters to me. Whether it's fostering meaningful relationships, pursuing a career that aligns with my passions, or making a positive impact in my community, I've identified the core values that guide my decisions and shape my vision for the future.

With my values as a compass, I've set concrete goals and milestones to work towards. Rather than drifting aimlessly through life, I've taken deliberate steps to chart my path and pursue my aspirations with purpose and determination. Whether it's advancing in my career, furthering my education, or nurturing my personal growth and development, each decision I make is informed by my overarching vision for the future.

But aligning my goals with my core values is just the first step—I've also learned the importance of taking purposeful action towards my future. This means setting SMART (Specific, Measurable, Achievable, Relevant, Time-bound) goals, breaking them down into actionable steps, and holding myself accountable for progress. Whether it's creating a budget to save for my dreams, networking with professionals in my field, or seeking out opportunities for growth and learning, I'm committed to taking consistent and intentional action to bring my vision to life.

Furthermore, I've embraced the concept of adaptability and flexibility in the pursuit of my goals. In a world that is constantly changing and evolving, I recognise that my path to success may not always be linear or straightforward. Rather than viewing setbacks or obstacles as failures, I see them as opportunities for growth and course correction. Whether it's pivoting to a new career path, reassessing my priorities, or learning from past mistakes, I'm committed to staying agile and resilient in the face of adversity.

As I approach my thirties, I do so with a sense of optimism and excitement for the future. By making informed decisions that are aligned with my core values and beliefs, and taking purposeful action towards my goals, I know that I am laying the foundation for a life of fulfilment, purpose, and abundance.

And as I continue on this journey of self-discovery and personal growth, I do so with the knowledge that my future is bright and full of possibilities, limited only by the boundaries of my imagination and the depths of my determination.

Key Takeaways:

- Your values are the guiding stars that illuminate your path, helping you navigate through life's twists and turns with authenticity and purpose.
- Reflecting on your values and beliefs is like fine-tuning the lens through which you view the world, allowing you to make decisions that resonate with your core self.
- Aligning goals with your core values is like crafting a compass that points you towards a future that feels truly authentic and fulfilling.

Action Steps:

- Conduct a values assessment. Write down five values that resonate with you deeply. How can you integrate them into your daily life, starting today?
- Take a moment to stand in front of an imaginary "values mirror." What do you see? How can you step through and embody those values in your actions and decisions?
- Begin working towards one goal that aligns with your core values. Remember, it's not about perfection, but progress. Each step forward is a victory.

ESSENTIAL LIFE TIPS FOR YOUR JOURNEY

- Research thoroughly before making big decisions; knowledge is your greatest ally in navigating the future.

- Consult mentors or experts; seeking advice can provide valuable perspectives and insights.

- Consider the long-term impact; weigh short-term gains against potential future consequences.

- Stay adaptable; the ability to pivot and adjust your plans is key in an ever-changing world.

- Set clear goals; having a vision for your future helps you make decisions that align with your aspirations.

EMPOWERING AFFIRMATIONS

- I trust my instincts and empower myself with the knowledge to make informed decisions for my future.

- Every choice I make is an investment in the life I want, and I approach decisions with clarity and confidence.

- I am the CEO of my life, weighing options carefully and steering towards a future that aligns with my vision.

- I embrace uncertainty as an opportunity for growth and use it to make strategic, forward-thinking decisions.

- I learn from every experience, turning lessons into wisdom that guides my decisions for a brighter future.

SAY THESE OUT LOUD!

Embrace Your Journey

Congratulations!!!

You've navigated the roadmap to self-discovery and growth, and now you stand at the threshold of an exciting new chapter.

Remember, this journey is not about reaching a final destination, but about relishing every step along the way. Embrace the challenges, celebrate the victories, and let each experience shape the masterpiece that is your life.

As you move forward, carry with you the wisdom gained from self-reflection, the courage to chase your dreams, and the belief that you hold the power to create a future that resonates with your truest self.

May your twenties be a time of bold choices, meaningful connections, and endless possibilities. Thrive, evolve, and never forget that you are the author of your own story.

Here's to a future filled with purpose, passion, and boundless potential. Keep thriving!

With heartfelt wishes,
Deandra Rose 🖤

30-Day Self Care Challenge

Take a 10-minute mindful walk	Write down 3 things you are grateful for	Cook a healthy meal for yourself	Spend 20 minutes meditating	Write a letter to your future self
Practice deep breathing for 10 minutes	Call or meet a friend for a heart-to-heart talk	Take a break from your mobile phone for the entire day	Try a new yoga pose	Take a long, relaxing bath
Visit a park or natural reserve	Listen to your favorite music	Spend time with a pet	Do a random act of kindness	Say "No" to a commitment you're not excited about
Write about a happy memory	Try a new hobby or revisit an old one	Watch your favorite movie	Go to bed half an hour earlier	Do something spontaneous
Buy yourself a small gift	Read a chapter of a book	Try a new tea or coffee flavor	Spend time in the sun	Write down 3 things you love about yourself
Practice mindfulness while doing a daily task	Take the day off chores and errands	Practice self-massage	Do something creative	Reflect on the progress you've made this month

Follow on Instagram for more:
@gracefulgrowthwithdee

www.ingramcontent.com/pod-product-compliance
Lightning Source LLC
Chambersburg PA
CBHW052059150726
48002CB00002B/951